D1165111

Ecosystems of North America

The Great Lakes

Sharon Katz

BENCHMARK BOOKS

MARSHALL CAVENDISH
NEW YORK

Series Consultant: Stephen R. Kellert, Ph.D., School of Forestry and Environmental Studies, Yale University

Consultant: Richard Haley, Director, Goodwin Conservation Center

Benchmark Books
Marshall Cavendish Corporation
99 White Plains Road
Tarrytown, New York 10591-9001

Library of Congress Cataloging-in-Publication Data

Katz, Sharon.
    The Great Lakes / Sharon Katz.
        p.   cm.—(Ecosystems of North America)
    Includes bibliographical references and index.
    Summary: Describes the formation of the Great Lakes, the varied life forms that are part of this ecosystem, the interactions among the plants and animals that live there, and threats to this environment.
    ISBN 0-7614-0898-3
    1. Ecology—Great Lakes—Juvenile literature. [1. Ecology—Great Lakes. 2. Freshwater ecology.]
    I. Title II. Series.
QH105.5.G7K38   1999   97-32693
577.68'0977—dc21   CIP
                                          AC

Photo Credits
The photographs in this book are used by permission and through the courtesy of:
Animals Animals/Earth Scenes: Ken Cole 14; R.H. Armstrong 21; Len Rue, Jr. 25; John Lemker 33, 40,56-57; Zia Leszczynski 34; J.H. Robinson 37; Marcia W. Griffen 49; Joe McDonald 51; Frank Roche 53. *Peter Arnold, Inc:* Carl R. Sams II front cover. *Photo Researchers, Inc:* A.W. Ambler 15; Scott Camazine 58. *Bob Simpson* 18-19. *Tom Stack & Associates:* Tom Algire 4-5, 10; Rod Planck 29,32; Terry Donnelly 41; Barbara Gerlach back cover. *Visuals Unlimited:* John Sohlden 8, 30; William Grenfell 12; Stephen W. Kress 22; Tom Edwards 28; John Sohlden 30; Roger A. Powell 38-39; Joe McDonald 42; Pat Armstrong 46-47. *Visuals Unlimited* 20. *Gene Wright* 26-27, 31. Cover design by Ann Antoshak for BBI.

Series Created and Produced by BOOK BUILDERS INCORPORATED

Printed in Hong Kong
6 5 4 3 2 1

Contents

Great Fresh-water Seas

Imagine standing on a sandy beach. You look out across water that spreads so far it seems to meet the sky. You make out tiny outlines of distant ships against the horizon. You hear the sound of waves crashing at your feet. A breeze blows sand against your cheeks. Is this an ocean shore? You sniff the moist air, but there is no scent of salt spray. This is not an ocean beach. You are looking at Lake Superior, part of the largest system of surface fresh water on Earth and one of North America's Great Lakes.

Why Are They Great Lakes?

The entire Great Lakes region is dominated and shaped by water, beginning with the five lakes themselves: Lake Erie, Lake Superior, Lake Huron, Lake Michigan, and Lake Ontario. They are shared by eight U.S. states—Minnesota, Wisconsin, Illinois, Michigan, Indiana, Ohio, Pennsylvania, and New York—and the provinces of Ontario and Quebec in Canada. The lakes cover 94,000 square miles (245,000 sq km) and contain 18 percent of the world's total fresh water. Only the polar ice caps contain more fresh water, but in frozen form. Lake Superior,

Beach grasses anchor dune sands on the shore of Lake Michigan.

the largest of the lakes, is 350 miles (560 km) long and averages 485 feet (150 m) deep. Lake Erie is the smallest: 240 miles (386 km) long with an average depth of only 62 feet (20 m). Together the lakes span about 750 miles (1,200 km) from west to east and contain 5,500 cubic miles (22,900 cubic km) of water. Their huge size means that they affect all aspects of the region, including temperature, rainfall, habitat, and wildlife.

Thousands of rivers, streams, smaller lakes, and ponds are connected directly and indirectly to the Great Lakes. Millions of birds, fish, and mammals make this area their home. The communities of plants and animals linked to each other and to the features of the Great Lakes form an **ecosystem**. A **community** refers to all of the organisms that live together and interact in a particular environment. An organism's **environment** is all of the living and nonliving things that surround the organism and affect its life. The study of communities of living things and the cycles they are a part of is called **ecology**. The ecology of the Great Lakes ecosystem is largely a study of water—its history, its effects, its cycles, and its connection to land and air.

Ice Moves across the Land

Imagine a large part of North America completely covered in massive sheets of ice called glaciers. The Great Lakes were formed through the movements of those glaciers thousands of years ago. The land where the Great Lakes took shape had already been pushed deeper than surrounding areas by ancient seas millions of years before. As the glaciers retreated toward the Arctic, where they remain today, they scraped out large chunks of land, leaving even deeper depressions. And because the ice was up to 6,500 feet (2,000 m) thick, its weight caused the land to sink lower, much like the depression you can make if you press your thumb into a piece of clay. When the climate began to warm up, the glaciers melted. A mile of melting ice can leave a huge puddle, and it did. The water ran to the lowest places, filling up the depressions in the land. There was so much melted ice that these areas eventually turned into the Great Lakes.

The Great Lakes

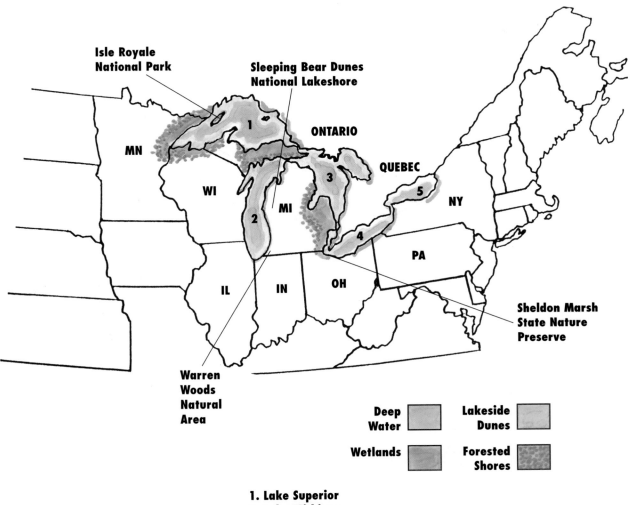

Isle Royale
National Park

Sleeping Bear Dunes
National Lakeshore

ONTARIO

QUEBEC

MN

WI

MI

IL

IN

OH

PA

NY

5

1

2

3

4

Sheldon Marsh
State Nature
Preserve

Warren
Woods
Natural
Area

Deep
Water

Lakeside
Dunes

Wetlands

Forested
Shores

1. Lake Superior
2. Lake Michigan
3. Lake Huron
4. Lake Erie
5. Lake Ontario

The five Great Lakes are shared by eight American states and two Canadian provinces.

Glaciers shaped the land as well. They dragged along a great quantity of rocks, sand, and silt with them. Over time, this debris was broken down to become fertile soil along the southern shores of Lake Michigan, Lake Erie, and Lake Ontario. And rich soil meant that huge forests could grow, which in turn supported large populations of wildlife, such as moose, coyotes, wolves, red foxes, and deer.

The glaciers also brought unique features to the land—deep grooves, narrow ridges called **eskers**, **moraines** (massive ridges formed from glacial meltwater debris), **kames** (cone-shaped mounds),

As glaciers retreated, they left many ridges and grooves, like this moraine in Michigan.

and many smaller lakes and ponds. When lakes or ponds fill in with sediments, they become marshes and bogs with specialized plant and animal communities. And because the lakes are so big, they have long shores with sloping stretches of sand called **dunes**.

How Does an Ecosystem Work?

Continuous movements called cycles are the defining parts of any ecosystem. Water, in its many changing forms, is essential. It evaporates from lakes, oceans, and land to form water vapor. Water vapor is a gas. It mixes with air and, like air, is invisible. But even though we cannot see it, we can feel it, especially on a warm summer day, when water vapor makes air feel damp. Warm air holds more vapor than cool air. Yet there is a limit to how much water vapor even warm air can hold. The air becomes saturated. The overabundance of water vapor condenses to form clouds, large masses of droplets in the air, which you can see. If clouds are close to the ground, we call them fog. If they are higher up in the sky, we call them clouds. Sometimes, clouds drop their moisture, and we see those droplets again as rain, sleet, or snow. This is how water returns to the earth's surface. The movement from land to air to land again is the **water cycle**, and it plays a crucial role in every ecosystem.

Yet water does more than move from land to air and back again. Think about how water flows. If rain falls directly onto a lake, it immediately becomes part of the lake. Often, though, water falls on land. It may eventually find its way to the lake too, but first the water must filter through soil and rock. Then it flows into streams and rivers, which in turn feed into the lake.

Water may fall on land made of different types of soils and surfaces. Sandy or rocky soils allow water to pass through them. You can see a similar filtering effect if you hold your open fingers under a faucet. If you clench your fingers tightly and watch water fall on your hand, you will notice that instead of falling through, the water gathers and then rolls off. The same thing happens if water falls on denser soil, such as clay, or on solid rock. It will bounce off and roll downward as **surface runoff**. The water may flow slowly or fast, depending on how much plant life it finds on its journey. The more

Streams bring water, nutrients, sediments, and plant and animal life to the Great Lakes.

plants in the soil, the more their roots tend to cling to moist soil and slow the water's speed.

Water not only connects the earth's surface to the air, it also links all the surface areas around the Great Lakes. Water can do this because it moves not only itself but also the organisms that live in it. Rivers and streams continuously bring new water and nutrients into the lakes. These **tributaries** provide spawning areas for fish, such as lake trout, and stopping places for migratory birds, such as sandhill cranes. Tributaries depend on vegetation. Vegetation regulates the amount of nutrients flowing into the tributaries. Root systems hold onto water and take up nutrients into plants. Without vegetation, more nutrients flow directly into the water. As it flows along its path toward the lakes, water can also pick up anything in its way, including rocks, soil, chemicals, and even plants and animals.

Energy Makes It All Run

As important as water is, it is only one of many elements in an ecosystem. Like all ecosystems, the Great Lakes is a large natural engine. It is fueled by energy from the sun. Soil, water, plants, and animals capture and soak up this energy. Green plants—from water lilies to sugar maples—use the sun's energy to make their own food. Animals such as squirrels, beavers, and frogs eat these plants to gain energy of their own. When these plants and animals die, they release their energy back into the environment with the help of **decomposers**, such as bacteria and fungi. Decomposers break down the dead plants and animals into nutrients, which return to the soil, where new plants can use them to grow. The energy continues to flow.

Both the flow of energy and cycling of water contribute to the **climate** of the Great Lakes. Although weather in the area may differ from day to day, the pattern of rainfall, temperature, and wind over a long time makes up the climate. The lakes absorb a huge amount of energy directly from the sun. Water heated by the sun in summer takes a long time to cool down. As a result, the air above the water's surface is warmer. In some areas around the lakes, this air helps keep winter from being too cold. In the summer, the reverse happens —cool air above the lakes' surface moderates the summer's heat.

Energy and water are interconnected. Temperatures in the system, for example, affect the water cycle. Warmer temperatures tend to cause more water evaporation. If the air is cooler, water evaporates more slowly. The Great Lakes are affected by warm, humid air from the Gulf of Mexico and also by cold, dry air from northern, arctic regions.

Living in the Neighborhood

Communities of plants and animals have gathered in the Great Lakes ecosystem and adjusted to the rainfall, temperature, and other climatic features available to them. They have **adaptations** for the Great Lakes physical environment—behaviors and bodies that help them survive. A beaver, for example, is well adapted for life in water. It has thick, waterproof fur, webbed feet for swimming, and transparent eyelids like goggles for seeing underwater.

Having chewed down small trees to build a dam, this beaver helped create a pond.

Animals such as the beaver are not only adapted to their surroundings, they also change those surroundings. Beavers create their own ponds within the Great Lakes ecosystem. When they build dams that form ponds, they affect many other organisms, some positively and some negatively. For example, beavers chew down trees for their dams. That means they often kill those trees they chew, but at the same time, they create gaps in the nearby forest, which allow more light to reach the forest floor. An increased amount of light means that the trees that beavers like most, such as aspen and birch, can grow.

Ponds created by beaver dams also provide **habitat**—the food, water, and shelter that organisms need to survive—for other plants and animals, such as duckweed and frogs. Plants here may have strong smells and bright colors to attract insects, such as bees and butterflies. Insects spread plant pollen while feeding, which helps the plants reproduce. Animals use the canals formed by beaver dams like highways to get from one place to another. They may also use the plants surrounding the dam to build nests. One beaver pond is thus a source of numerous relationships among living organisms—a complex biological community.

Animals use all parts of the ecosystem in different ways. Although some animals, such as deepwater fish, stay in only one part of the Great Lakes, other animals use many parts of the system. The lakes' hooded merganser, a waterbird, hatches in a tree cavity on a forested shore. It spends its youth in the sheltered shallows of a river leading to the lake or on a protected shore. When it is old enough to feed, it takes to the open water in search of fish.

People Enter the System

Ecosystems are not static—they are in constant flux. Ecosystems composed largely of water, such as the Great Lakes, are especially changeable. Because there is so much movement of water, animals, and even plants, the health of any one part of the ecosystem is dependent on the health of all the other parts. This is where humans enter the picture. Over the past three hundred years, people have become the most influential element in the system.

Hooded mergansers are raised on the shallow shores and feed on the open lake when they are grown.

About 32 million people live in the Great Lakes region. The lakes are a source of drinking water, fish, and other food; they provide power for homes and industries and a place for recreation. People depend on the lakes. The lakes, in turn, depend on people, who must learn to be wise caretakers. In the past, we have not always been so. Some of our actions have created pollutants and excess nutrients, many of which end up in the lakes. If nutrients or pollutants enter the system on the northern shores of the lakes, they will not stay there. In just a few days, those nutrients or pollutants can be found in the middle of Lake Erie or on the far southern shores of the system.

Although substances can move through the water, they can also become part of living communities through the **food chain—**

the series of organisms that eat each other. In the Great Lakes, for example, phytoplankton are eaten by zooplankton, which are in turn eaten by smelt. Because of this constant feeding, nutrients and pollutants are transmitted through the system. The consequences can be both good and bad. Every living thing needs nitrogen and phosphorus. Fish, reptiles, birds, and mammals receive these critical nutrients from the plants and animals they eat. But pollutants can also travel through the ecosystem in this same way and have far-reaching effects on its plant and animal communities. How does this movement occur? If a tiny one-celled animal eats too much DDT (a human-made chemical once widely used for pest control), eventually an eagle will also ingest that DDT. The eagle will have a lot more of it in its body because chemicals like DDT do not readily break apart in animals' digestive systems. These chemicals become more concentrated as they move through the food chain. That concentrating process is called **bioaccumulation**.

American white pelicans are at the top of the Great Lakes food chain.

Bioaccumulation means that if a tiny plant, such as the **phytoplankton**, absorbs water with a very small amount of an industrial chemical, only that small amount is in the plant. A small animal, a **zooplankton**, may eat many of those plants. The zooplankton consumes all the tiny amounts of chemicals combined from all the plants it ate. When a fish comes along and eats zooplankton, the combined amount of chemicals accumulates in its body. The process continues. At each step up the food chain, as larger animals eat smaller animals, chemicals like DDT bioaccumulate in animals' bodies.

Animals at the top of the food chain, such as eagles and ospreys, can actually have huge amounts of industrial toxins in their bodies simply from their normal diets, even if the water near their homes has very little. When the eagles and ospreys die, the toxins do not disappear. Decomposers go to work breaking them apart, and soon those chemicals return to the water and to the soil, remaining in the system for a very long time. As you will see in the following chapters, the cycle of biaccumulation shows how dependent all parts of the ecosystem are on each other.

In this book you will visit the open lake at Lake Erie, the wetlands of Sheldon Marsh State Nature Preserve, the dunes at Sleeping Bear Dunes National Lakeshore, and the forests at Isle Royale National Park and Warren Woods. You will explore interactions among members of these biological communities and learn to recognize their distinctive adaptations. You will begin to understand that many organisms—including humans—are truly interdependent within this ecosystem.

Humans have always used the lakes for transportation. The Erie Canal was built in 1825 to carry early settlers west and transport goods from the east. Canals linking all the lakes were built throughout the nineteenth century, as the population grew and industry expanded. By 1959, the St. Lawrence Seaway had been built, allowing large ocean vessels access to the Great Lakes.

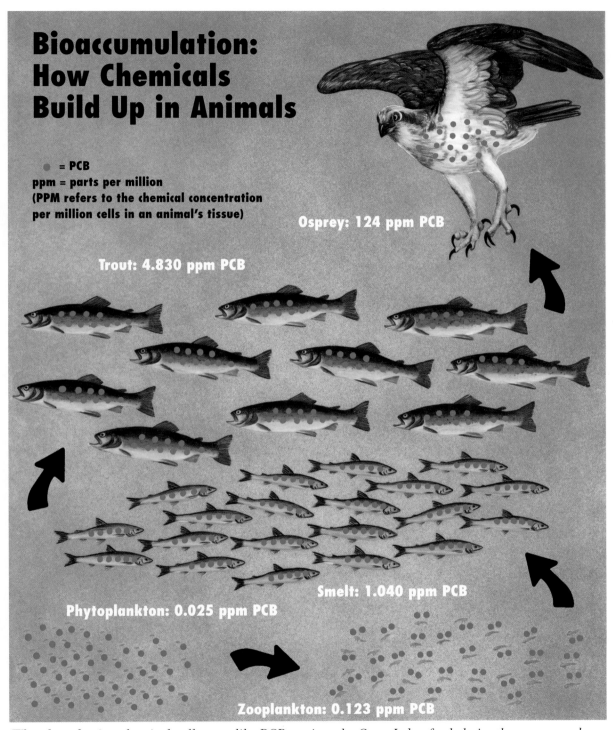

Bioaccumulation: How Chemicals Build Up in Animals

● = PCB
ppm = parts per million
(PPM refers to the chemical concentration
per million cells in an animal's tissue)

Osprey: 124 ppm PCB

Trout: 4.830 ppm PCB

Smelt: 1.040 ppm PCB

Phytoplankton: 0.025 ppm PCB

Zooplankton: 0.123 ppm PCB

When long-lasting chemical pollutants like PCB get into the Great Lakes food chain, they are passed along from organism to organism until they accumulate in the animals at the top of that chain. When an animal like the osprey dies and decomposes, the accumulated PCB in its body re-enters the food chain.

To Eat or Be Eaten

*O*ut in the middle of Lake Erie, the water seems quiet and still. Yet there is a lot going on below the surface. It is here that many of the life cycles in and around the Great Lakes begin. There are not as many **species**, or kinds, of plants and animals out here in the deep water as there are on and near the shore. Nevertheless, those species that survive in open waters are essential to making the rest of the system work.

Light for Life

Lake water is not uniform from top to bottom. Its qualities vary with depth. In the deepest layer, it is cold and dark. Where there is no light, no plants can grow. Lake Erie is about 60 feet (20 m) deep and the shallowest of the Great Lakes. Even so, sunlight can reach down only about 45 feet (15 m). In the lighted layer of the water, where there are also nutrients such as phosphorus and nitrogen, phytoplankton—or algae—soak up the sunlight. They use the sun's energy and nutrients to produce their own food and to reproduce in a process called **photosynthesis**.

Commercial fishers catch smelt and other fish in Lake Erie.

18

Zooplankton feed on algae in the open lake.

Algae float on the surface of the water in huge groups and move with the currents. But they are not alone out here. Tiny animals called zooplankton use the water's movements and their small tentacles to come near these floating algae. Zooplankton often look much like algae; the only real difference is that they cannot photosynthesize on their own. Instead, they feed hungrily on the algae near the surface of the water. These minuscule plants and animals—together known as plankton—form the basis of the food chain. They provide meals for fish, turtles, birds, and countless other creatures.

Many small fish feed on plankton. For example, shad, smelt, and sunfish are plankton feeders that search the water for tasty mouthfuls. And in turn, these fish are eaten by bigger fish, such as lake trout, lake sturgeon, and northern pike. The pike is a skilled hunter, or **predator**. It hunts with patience, moving very slowly until it is within range of its prey. At striking range, it flicks its powerful tail, darts quickly, and in a flash, captures its next meal. The pike and other predator fish spend most of their lives in open water, where they can find prey. However, they swim to shallower waters and rivers to spawn. Trout hollow out a small space on a rocky shoreline to lay thousands of eggs. Only a few eggs survive to adulthood. The rest make meals for crabs, crayfish, and other shallow-bottom feeders.

Predators, Human and Wild

Above the lake, birds of prey scan the waters with sharp eyes for the flash of fish scales. An osprey or bald eagle will swoop down to scoop up a fish in the blink of an eye. Ospreys nest in high tree branches on forested shores, but they feed from the air. An osprey may dive to the water, scoop up a trout, and eat it as a take-out meal on the way back to its nest. These birds, along with humans, are the top predators in the open lake food chain.

The northern pike eats many smaller fish.

The osprey, a fish eater, was threatened by high levels of DDT in its body.

The osprey's diet is made up largely of fish. As a result, pollutants in the fish are magnified in the bird's body through the process of bioaccumulation. Scientists have discovered that high concentrations of the pesticide DDT in the bodies of ospreys cause eggshell thinning. When eggs have weak shells, they break easily and hatchlings cannot survive. This problem caused a severe decline in the osprey population in the 1970s. Fortunately, DDT has been banned in many areas of the world, and osprey populations are recovering.

While ospreys and eagles snatch fish from the water's surface, plankton not eaten by fish die there. Their bodies drift slowly to the lower layers of the water and eventually to the bottom. There, in the darkness, **benthic organisms**—such as the bottom-feeding whitefish—eat the dead plankton and use their nutrients for energy. So the deep waters provide food not only for those animals that can swim to the surface, but also for those living near the bottom.

Humans have been catching fish in the Great Lakes since the 1820s. Commercial fishers caught the most fish ever in the late 1800s, harvesting 147 million pounds (67 million kg) of lake trout, sturgeon, blue pike, and Atlantic salmon per year. They were careless about how much they harvested. Their catches were too big and too frequent. As a result, fish could not reproduce themselves fast enough to keep up. This meant that harvests soon began to decline. One entire category of deepwater fish, known as ciscoes, were nearly driven to extinction by overfishing. Now the commercial fishery is mostly made up of species such as smelt and alewife, introduced to the lakes by humans. These species are worth a lot less than the predatory fish that once roamed the lakes in such great numbers. Only small areas of the lakes remain profitable for fishing.

Problems and Solutions

All of the plants and animals in the open water depend closely on each other through their food chain. Pollution affecting one kind of organism soon affects others. Pollution produced by people is a major problem for the lakes, and for Lake Erie especially. There are many kinds of pollutants, and they come from different places. They can be PCBs, which are chemicals from industrial plants that wash in from rivers and streams feeding the lake. They can be acids or carbon dioxide, brought in on the wind and settling onto the water's surface. And they can even be too much of generally good things! For example, in small quantities phosphorus is essential to all organisms' survival, but too much phosphorus can cause big problems. Phosphorus is a major ingredient of fertilizers, and it can wash into the lakes from farmlands.

Pollution is a problem because pollutants may stop plant and animal bodies from functioning normally, or they may put living systems out of balance. Pollutants are generally not serious in small quantities. But in the Great Lakes, they accumulate because water moves out of the lakes very slowly.

Lake Erie showed the first serious signs of illness in the middle of the twentieth century when it came down with a "disease" called **eutrophication**. Eutrophication occurs when excess nutrients cause algae to multiply much faster than normal. When these huge amounts of algae die and sink to the bottom of the

Lake Superior is the largest of the Great Lakes. It could contain all of the other great Lakes and an additional three Lake Eries! It contains 2,900 cubic miles (12,083 cubic km) of water. If all the water evaporated from Lake Superior, it would take 191 years to replace it!

lake to decompose, they use up dissolved oxygen in the water. As oxygen levels in the lake fall, fish can no longer get enough oxygen from the water into their gills. As a result, they die. Predatory fish and birds soon discover they have little prey left to eat. The food chain begins to fall apart. Lake Erie suffered from this problem first because it is surrounded by the most agriculture and development, and also because it is the smallest and shallowest of the Great Lakes.

Another major problem in the open lake has been the introduction of **exotic species**, those not native to the area. Because so many parts of an ecosystem are interconnected, an exotic species can disrupt relationships and bring unpredictable changes to the whole ecosystem.

Zebra mussels, for example, are tiny striped shellfish that arrived in the Great Lakes undetected. They probably had been sucked into the ballast water of a ship from the Caspian Sea in western Asia. When the ship came to the Great Lakes and dumped its ballast water, the zebra mussels found a new home with no natural predators—species that would eat them and control their numbers. Just one female zebra mussel can produce hundreds of thousands of eggs, so it is easy to see how rapidly the population of these invaders rose. Zebra mussels entered Lake Erie during the late 1980s. Within a few years they had grown so abundant that they were clogging water-intake pipes and attaching themselves to boat hulls, causing billions of dollars of damage.

Zebra mussels also pose a threat to native species. They eat enormous quantities of phytoplankton, taking over the food supply of native Great Lakes clams and mussels. Zebra mussels have eaten so much algae, in fact, that large sections of Lake Erie are entirely clear. This effect seems positive, especially because the overabundant, pollution-fed algae had reduced the oxygen in the lake needed by other species. But ecologists wonder what will happen to the zooplankton that need the vanished algae as a food supply. And there may be an impact on the walleye, the best-known game fish of Lake Erie, which feed on zooplankton. It is difficult to predict the consequences with certainty.

Zebra mussels, shown here exposed at low tide, have multiplied out of control.

To address pollution and exotic species problems, scientists and concerned residents came up with a plan to restore the lakes by lowering levels of pollutants in the system. They developed the Great Lakes Water Quality Agreement. It states that all the people who use the lakes must work together to control pollution levels. Scientists identify where the pollutants are coming from and make suggestions about how to stop them from entering the lakes. These suggestions include installing water treatment plants, monitoring water quality, doing research, controlling emissions of phosphorus in the water, and eliminating the release of toxic chemicals from industrial plants. The agreement was first signed in 1972 and has been renewed several times. The good news is that because of cooperation and dedication, the effects of pollution are declining. Many species are recovering, and people can once again enjoy the natural beauty and benefits of the lakes.

Soggy Roots and Webbed Feet

Flying swiftly several hundred feet above the ground, a cormorant scans the land for a suitable resting place. Tired from its flight, it needs to alight soon to find food and conserve energy. A shallow pond with cattails clustered around the edges catches the cormorant's eye. The bird slows its wing beats. It comes in for a splash landing and finds a muddy bank that makes a good resting spot. The pond offers ample fish for dinner.

This cormorant has found a resting place in one of the richest wildlife habitats—a **wetland**. There are many kinds of wetlands, but they are all areas where the water level is above or near the land surface for at least part of the year. Wetlands around the Great Lakes may be marshes or bogs. Marshes are warm coastal wetlands, and bogs are colder inland wetlands. Each is home to a distinct community of animals and plants.

Sheldon Marsh is a great place to see thousands of birds heading north on their spring migration.

Double-crested cormorants dive into the water to catch fish and return to the surface to eat them.

Sheldon Marsh State Nature Preserve is on the coast of Lake Erie. It is one of Ohio's last coastal wetlands and provides a home for more than three hundred species of birds. Coastal marshes like this one buffer inland areas from changing water levels. Open lake water delivers nutrients to the marsh and returns nutrients to the lake. This continual replenishing creates an inviting habitat for many different species.

How can you tell you are in a marsh? The easiest way is to look for dense vegetation in the water. Water plants capture the sun's light. As plants grow, they slow the water's movements, protect areas from wind, and collect sediments. Marsh plants have to be well adapted to constant water at their roots. Some are called **emergent plants**. They grow with their roots in water for part or all of their lives. Emergent plants include sedges and cattails. Cattails are everywhere in a marsh! They push up through shallow waters and create a food supply for insects and mammals. They provide shelter for nests of waterbirds and semiaquatic mammals.

Floating-leaf plants have leaves that float on the water's surface. The water lily is one example. Its roots reach through deep water and send broad leaves to the surface. Nutrients move between the leaves and roots through thin stems, 5 to 6 feet (1.5–2 m) long. **Submergent plants**, such as pondweeds and bladderworts, have stems, leaves, and roots mostly underwater. They are highly sensitive and can gather light even in murky water. Submergent plants often flower at the water's surface. These plants make excellent food for ducks.

Floating plants are not rooted in one place. They float on the water's surface and get their nutrients directly from the water. Duckweed and water hyacinth are floating plants.

Dense vegetation in the marsh attracts numerous birds looking for food. Water-based vegetation soaks up the nutrients. The vegetation may also soak up chemical pollutants in the water, beginning the cycle of bioaccumulation. When birds eat these plants, pollutants accumulate in their bodies.

Sheldon Marsh also provides habitat for nesting, rearing young, and feeding. Marsh birds specialize on different kinds of plants. Grebes nest at water level. Coots and rails use low vegetation

Cattails, which provide food and nesting materials for muskrats and other animals, thrive in a wetland.

Duckweed is one of several floating plants found in marshes.

near water level. Egrets feed on cattails, and wood ducks use trees at the edge of the marsh. Green herons feed on fish and amphibians and may eat other bird's eggs, snakes, or small rodents when the opportunity arises. Herons sometimes cheat when looking for food. They will follow a grebe, using it as an indicator for the location of good fish. When a fish escapes from a grebe, the heron swoops down to grab it. So each kind of bird has its own special ecological **niche**, or its space and role within the habitat.

Birds are abundant, but they are not alone in Sheldon Marsh. Fish such as hefty carp grow and feed in the protection of marsh vegetation. At the water's edge here, an old field waving with red clover and milkweed is home to munching monarch caterpillars. In mid-September, as adult monarch butterflies prepare for their annual migration to Mexico, they return to their old feasting grounds to sip clover nectar. On a log by the cattails, a row of painted turtles soaks up the sun's energy. Painted turtles are reptiles. Like all reptiles, they cannot produce their own heat. So painted turtles gather in shallow marsh water to heat their bodies. Painted turtles find food easily here, especially since they will eat just about anything— animal or vegetable.

Many land animals avoid water, but several have adapted to the marsh to take advantage of its rich protein sources. The muskrat is a large rodent with dense fur, a long scaly tail, and partially webbed feet. It depends heavily on cattails, not only for food, but also for shelter. The muskrat builds its nest with piles and piles of cattails on top of a mud and branch foundation.

Beavers are also among the few mammals that are marsh specialists. To compensate for changing water levels, they create their own ponds by chewing down nearby trees and building dams. Around the edge of a marsh, skunks, raccoons, ground squirrels, mink, and even deer lurk. As night falls on Sheldon Marsh, the low mating calls of the leopard frog and American toad pulse through the humid air.

Wetlands improve water quality because they filter out and modify sediments, nutrients, and pollutants. The water that has flowed through a marsh returns cleaner to the surrounding area and eventually seeps into the groundwater. Marshes provide this

Elegant egrets and other water-birds feed on cattails, fish, and amphibians in Sheldon Marsh.

31

service much more cheaply than the water treatment plants that humans install along the coasts. They also prevent erosion, help control flooding, and provide spawning areas and thousands of niches for wildlife.

What's in a Bog?

Unlike marshes, which are warm, humid, and filled with life, bogs are colder wetlands. A bog is a quiet place. The air feels cool. Bogs are cooler than surrounding areas because they were formed originally by the remains of glacial retreat. Sunken land pushed down by large chunks of melting ice became cold pools—the birthplace of bogs.

Sedge grasses grow from the banks of the pool, spreading into the center to form a floating mat. Sphagnum moss grows on this mat. Shrubs grow on top when the mat is thick enough. Water below is cold and acidic, like lemon juice, and inhospitable

This cold, dew-laden bog was formed when sunken land was pushed down by large chunks of melting ice from glaciers.

The pitcher plant drowns its insect prey in rain water caught in its tube-shaped leaves.

to organisms that normally break down plant remains. The mat thickens and thickens. Eventually, the bottom and top layers meet. A bog mat sinks gently underfoot. Walking through a bog is like stepping on foam rubber.

Sphagnum moss is the main ingredient in a bog. It acts like a giant sponge. The top layer is living, while the lower layer is dead and quite sterile. The lower layer is often called peat moss, a soil made of slightly decomposed plant bodies. Peat moss used to be harvested by humans to burn as fuel.

Female four-toed salamanders lay their eggs close to each other so they can take turns watching them.

As peat builds up, nutrients, water, and energy become locked up with dead plant bodies. Less available energy and fewer nutrients mean growth is slow. Nutrients cannot cycle as actively as they do in other wetlands, and limited numbers of organisms can live here. Plants have to be very specialized. Believe it or not, bog plants must have adaptations similar to those found in deserts, where water is precious. Desert plants must develop strategies to hold onto water, and bog plants, too, must hold onto every drop of good water in their harshly acidic surroundings. Bog plants often have tough coatings or woolly undersides to keep water vapor from evaporating.

Plants That Hunt

To gain additional nutrients, some plants have developed a very special adaptation—they are meat eaters! Because they cannot move around to hunt for food, each species of meat-eating, or **carnivorous**, plant has developed its own method of trapping insects and other small creatures. For example, the pitcher plant has a vaselike structure with a slippery surface. Insects attracted to the sweet smell of the plant lose their footing and slide down. In the bottom of the vase, they are digested by enzymes and bacteria. These bacteria break down the insects' bodies into a liquid so that nutrients can be absorbed by the plant. Other animals take advantage of the pitcher plant's meat-eating techniques. Mosquito larva hang by the pitcher plant's entrance and snatch insects attracted by the aroma. Spiders weave webs across the mouth of the vase, and tree frogs wait nearby. All hope to snag an easy meal without falling in.

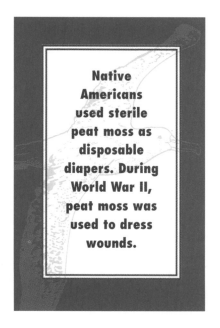

Native Americans used sterile peat moss as disposable diapers. During World War II, peat moss was used to dress wounds.

Amphibians at Home

Although the bog is a harsh environment, some creatures have adapted to take advantage of it. The reddish-brown four-toed salamander thrives in the bog beneath the sphagnum moss. Amphibians breathe through their skin, so they need moisture to help transfer oxygen into their bodies. The wetness of the bog allows them to do this. Female four-toed salamanders each lay their two to three dozen eggs in thick bog moss close to each other. In one site there can be up to 1,100 eggs! The females then take turns guarding these eggs, like cooperative baby-sitting.

When the eggs hatch about seven weeks later, baby salamanders, or larvae, squirm out of the jellied egg mass and drop into the cool water. Larvae spend the first month and a half of their lives here, breathing through gills and swimming in the bog's central water. When they transform, or metamorphose, into adults, they lose gills and fins. In their place salamanders grow legs and the four toes on their rear feet that give them their name.

As adults, they live secretively, wriggling quietly in the protection of the sphagnum moss under the cover of night. But if a predator does find one, it is in for a surprise. Four-toeds can break off their tails where the tail attaches to the body. The tail will skitter off by itself, drawing attention and distracting the predator, while the salamander scurries quickly into the moss. The tail will regrow shortly.

Draining the Wetlands

Humans have left large footprints across the wetlands of the Great Lakes. Wetlands may be thriving with plant and animal communities, but they are also popular places for buildings. In fact, over two-thirds of Great Lakes wetlands have been drained for development and agriculture. Because the wetlands provide spawning areas for Great Lakes fish and prevent erosion and flooding, their elimination has destroyed much wildlife in the region.

However, recovery has begun. Cormorants and bald eagles are making a comeback along the coasts of Lake Erie and Lake Superior. The bald eagle population fell rapidly in the 1950s and 1960s. The cause was DDT, a chemical used in agriculture to control pests. This pesticide bioaccumulated, leading to weak eggshells and contamination of the birds' food sources. Scientists estimate that in the 1700s there were as many as 75,000 breeding pairs of eagles in the Lower Forty-eight states. By the early 1960s there were fewer than 450 nesting pairs. They were officially

Bladderworts are a group of submergent plants that actually resemble both underwater monsters and submarines. The bladderwort is a floating carnivore with tiny bladders that trap unsuspecting insects beneath the water's surface. At the same time, it also has a beautiful yellow flower that it sends to the surface as a periscope.

declared endangered in 1967, and DDT was banned in 1972. The ban along with captive breeding programs have led to a remarkable recovery. There are now more than 4,000 breeding pairs, many nesting by the marshes and bogs of the Great Lakes.

Bald eagles have had a remarkable recovery from the brink of extinction.

Shifting Sands

On the northeastern shore of Lake Michigan lies Sleeping Bear Dunes National Lakeshore. Here the ghostlike forms of gnarled trees reach up, etching the solid blue sky with their branches. These dead trees, swept forever by shifting sands, stand watch over the largest system of freshwater dunes in the world. Dunes are stretches of sandy landscape formed when currents of wind and water drive sand and sediments upland from the beaches. These sands accumulate against trees and rocks, forming drifts over time. When sands reach a group of trees, they slowly replace the soil, killing the trees. On the Great Lakes, dunes can be found largely on the eastern shores of Lake Michigan.

Animals and plants must adapt to a landscape that changes with shifting sands. By examining living communities, scientists can judge how long the dunes have been here and how recently changes have occured. **Succession** parades through the dune communities, as one group of organisms replaces another. Each group helps provide the right conditions for the next. For example, marram grass anchors sand, which eventually forms a sandy soil. This soil allows

Blowing sands bury nutrients too deep for roots to reach, leaving ghostly forests in their path.

Marram grass stabilizes sand and paves the way for other species to take hold.

other kinds of plants to grow, which in turn attracts animals that eat them. Near the water's edge, there is little but sand, while farthest away, dunes may be completely covered with trees.

First to Take Root

On a stretch of bare sand, little can live until a hardy species takes hold. Marram grass seeds are blown by the wind and eventually settle down to send sturdy roots into the sand. To withstand wind, the grass must depend on the anchoring power of those roots, which can grow up to 20 feet (6 m) long underground. The roots spread under the sand's surface, sending up shoots like a submarine periscope every few inches. Like the steel skeletons underlying layers of concrete in a tall building, marram grass roots provide a framework to hold the sand in place.

Above ground, marram grass sends up slender stalks. Sand piles grow and grow, but so does the grass, doing its best to stay just one step ahead of the sand. To keep its pores from filling with sand and prevent moisture from escaping, blades curl in to form a strawlike cylinder.

Living on the Dunes

In a sense, marram grass tames the sand and makes it habitable for other organisms. Once the grasses have done their job, less adventurous plants begin to find their places. Sand cherry, grape,

A beech-maple forest takes hold in an old, sandy dune.

and poison ivy vines take hold, further anchoring sandy soil. These vines and small shrubs add their nutrients to the soil. Their roots hold water and attract small animals, such as worms and snails, that are essential to good soil. After the animals die, decomposers go to work converting their bodies back into nutrients. Sheltered areas form beyond the front of a dune where winds are not as intense. Here woody plants such as northern bayberry and beach plum provide shade. Farther inland, groups of cottonwood trees and jack pines grow, and even farther inland there are black oak forests. Groups of beech and maple trees are sure signs of an old and stable dune.

With each successional stage, there is also a change in the animal community. In addition to worms transforming the soil, vines and shrubs attract other animal explorers. Humans may run from

The piping plover is a highly endangered resident of Lake Michigan.

poison ivy's telltale reddish, three-pointed leaves, but sixty species of birds feed on poison ivy berries! Woodpeckers depend on them in the winter when their insect food is not around. Ponds in the dunes provide habitat for herons, bufflehead ducks, and soft-shell turtles. The heron is an important predator in the dune community. It feeds on fish and frogs but will also eat rodents, reptiles, and once in awhile, a small bird. As a top predator in the dune food chain, herons are especially vulnerable to the cycle of bioaccumulation, and toxins taken up from plants and smaller animals can be dangerous to their health.

Winds and waves provide a constant challenge for animals. The dune food chain starts when waves bring in a pile of protein sources—bits of dead fish, vegetation, snail bodies, insects, and plankton. Careful to avoid being washed away themselves, crabs and crayfish dash to the water's edge to take advantage of this special-delivery meal. Herons and other long-legged birds pace shorelines searching for crabs and crayfish, along with other tasty morsels.

Migratory birds use these dunes as a stopping place in their travels. The piping plover is an endangered species that nests along Great Lakes shores, particularly in this area of Michigan. In the fall, it migrates to the Gulf of Mexico. The plover is a small, sand-colored shorebird with orange legs. It depends on the dunes, where it feeds on insects, spiders, and crustaceans. As beaches were developed for cities and industries, plovers fled. By 1983, there were only a few dozen breeding pairs left. Now scientists and citizens are making special efforts to protect the piping plover's habitat.

Farther back from the water, dune grasses provide shelter for small rodents. The meadow vole burrows through the sands and makes its nest in the cool earth right beneath the surface. Coyotes and an occasional

Sandhill cranes stop along the dunes on their annual migration. These tall, distinctive blue-gray birds with red foreheads mate for life. Each spring cranes will engage their partners in elaborate balletlike dances, leaping many feet into the air. Though they were once highly threatened by habitat destruction, protected areas have allowed their population to rebound in recent years.

bobcat are top mammal predators. They seem to play hide and seek with the voles, as they search for their dinners.

Sleeping Bear Dunes is called a **blowout dune**. Wind or fire destroys vegetation that anchored the sand. Once vegetation is gone, wind tears a hole in the dune and throws the sand around. At Sleeping Bear, the hole formed a distinctive big bowl with arms. This dune served as a landmark for Native Americans and early French explorers. According to legend, a mother bear and her twin cubs were driven across Lake Michigan by a forest fire. When the mother bear reached the shore, she climbed onto a bluff to wait for her cubs, but they were so tired they drowned before reaching shore. Now, according to the legend, the cubs lie offshore as North and South Manitou Islands.

Development on the Delicate Beach

Humans have had a significant impact on the dunes. Natural storms cause damage through erosion and flooding, but well-anchored dune systems can withstand a lot of wind and water. When humans build near dunes, however, they often tear out vegetation. As a result, the sand no longer stays in place. This destruction happened extensively in the 1800s when steelmaking became a big business in the region. Steel mills on Lake Michigan needed to be near water for their industrial processes. Many beaches were ruined.

Shoreline recreation provides major economic benefits for the Great Lakes region, and thousands of tourists come each year seeking vacations. Tourism has had a major impact on dune systems. Many people living on the lakes have pleasure boats, and others seek solitude on dunes and beaches. Development for summer cottages, beaches, and boat docks has resulted in loss of dune and forested sections. Severe erosion has been one result. In addition, people disturb habitats and cause birds such as the piping plover to abandon their nests. In recent years, both the U.S. and Canadian governments have made attempts to set up pro-tected reserves and conservation areas, while still allowing people to enjoy the beaches.

Tracing Water's Path over Land

Materials:

- large rectangular aluminum baking pan (the disposable kind)
- sponges
- a couple of rocks
- leaves
- soil
- small plastic containers
- foil
- vegetable oil
- blue or green food coloring
- water

1. Go out into your neighborhood and collect some soil, rocks, grass, leaves, sticks—anything made by nature that looks interesting. Be sure not to take a lot of anything or disturb any animals.

2. Bring back your collection to your kitchen or backyard and arrange it in a large rectangular aluminum baking pan. Pile up rocks; put in a sponge in one part; add a little soil. Cover a plastic container with aluminum foil to make a bare hilltop. Make a pile of leaves to represent a tree. Try to make a little hill somewhere. Be creative.

3. When you are happy with your landscape, get a cup (or a watering can, if you have one) of water and add two or three drops of food coloring. (The food coloring just makes it easier to see, so do not worry if you do not have any.) Slowly pour the water, like rain, over your landscape. Watch where it goes and how fast it travels over each surface. If you want to do something extra, pour on a second cup of water, but this time add a few teaspoons of oil to the cup before you pour it. Watch what happens.

Questions to think about:
What surfaces does the water sink into?
What materials does the water bounce off of?
Where does water move most quickly or most slowly?
What kinds of ecosystem features does each of your mini-features represent?
What does this experiment tell you about the way land affects water's flow?

Shady Homes

*A*n eagle gliding swiftly inland from the open lake will pass over sand dunes and marshes and then come to forested shores—miles and miles of green treetops. The kinds of trees the eagle sees below depend on which shore it flies over. Descending through branches on the northern shores of the Great Lakes, the eagle will discover **conifer evergreens**. These are trees that grow needles, which they keep year-round, and store their seeds in cones. Conifer evergreens, such as jack pine and spruce, survive in thin, acidic soils. Pine and spruce drop layers of their needles onto the ground, eventually building up a thick, soft mat and providing a home for many living things.

If the eagle flies to the southern shores of the lakes, it will find forests of beech and maples. These forests are mostly **deciduous trees**, which lose their leaves in the fall. Beech trees can be giants! They usually form the very roof of the forest, called the **canopy**. The sugar maple, a shade-loving tree, lives in the **understory**, or lower level of the forest.

The largest region is the hemlock-white pine forest. Hemlocks need rich, moist soil. These evergreens alternate with deciduous and mixed forests,

Warren Woods is one of the few remaining old-growth forests, which used to cover all of the southern Great Lakes shores.

each group of trees finding a place where the soil is right. Each type of forest supports a community of other living organisms. Sometimes the organisms are highly specialized. For example, the Kirtland's warbler—a rare bird—is endangered because it nests in young jack pines, a tree that sprouts after forest fires. Logging practices stopped the cycle of natural fires. As a result, the habitat of the Kirtland's warbler disappeared. The U.S. Forest Service now runs controlled fires and grows special areas of young jack pines in the pine barrens of lower Michigan, to provide homes for this bird.

Still Going Strong

Although most of the Great Lakes' southern shores were once heavily forested with deciduous trees, they are covered no more. Logging, agriculture, and urban development have left their marks; most original forests have disappeared forever. But in one tiny corner of lower Michigan, on the eastern shore of Lake Michigan, beech-maple forest grows as it has for centuries, undisturbed by human industry. Warren Woods Natural Area has a canopy so thick that the forest temperature is cooler than in surrounding areas. Old-growth trees—those that have never been cut by humans—tower above, forming a green cathedral ceiling far overhead. Old-growth trees are usually bigger and taller than trees that have grown more recently in deforested areas. Large trees, surrounded by layers of fallen leaves, absorb a lot of sound. It is quiet here in the shadows of these majestic trees.

In the understory, maple seedlings sprout in every patch of ground where light finds the forest floor. Maples are patient trees. They will grow slowly as long as light is limited. But as soon as a storm fells a few large trees and creates a gap in the forest, they

It may be hard to believe, but trees can be tough competitors! Maple seeds sometimes find a way of digging through pine needle mats in mixed evergreen and deciduous forests. As soon as a big tree falls and allows maple seedlings to catch a little sunlight, they grow fast enough to cut off light from sun-loving birch seedlings. A mature mixed forest may hide dying birch seedlings on the forest floor, as they are slowly buried in needles.

The pileated woodpecker uses its bill to probe tree bark for an insect meal.

will speedily grow upward toward the promise of sun. Once at canopy level, maples can live up to four hundred years! They provide food and shelter for many kinds of wildlife.

Maples are also part of an important forest cycle. Their deep roots suck up nutrients from the soil far beneath the forest floor and pull them up to their leaves in the canopy. When the leaves fall, nutrients such as magnesium, calcium, and potassium remain inside them, and those leaves blanket the forest floor. Decomposer organisms quickly break down leaves to become part of the surface soil.

Maples, therefore, play an important role in cycling nutrients from lower levels of soil back to the top layers, where surface-dwelling organisms can use them. Once on the surface, animals and plants can get these nutrients into their bodies, where they use them for energy and growth.

Birds such as warblers, flycatchers, barred owls, and woodpeckers hide and feed among old-growth trees. Warblers sing their high-pitched, unique mating songs from gnarled branches, while owls hoot softly at dusk, searching for small rodents. Pileated wood-peckers hollow out distinctive rectangular nesting holes in tall trees. These holes can be as much as 3 feet (1 m) deep! From the nest, both male and female will go out on missions for ants, ant eggs, wood-boring beetles, larvae, berries, and even the seeds of their nesting tree.

Food and Shelter for Small Creatures

Eastern chipmunks avoid predators such as the barred owl by finding shelter among rocks, shrubs, seedlings, and loose soil in the forest. The chipmunks' light and dark stripes are adaptations that allow them to hide among patches of sun and shade on the forest floor. Chipmunks spend most of their time finding food, shaving off sharp edges of seeds and nuts, and stuffing them into their cheek pouches. Then they deposit their goodies into their very own pantries—stores of food that can hold up to 1.5 gallons (6 l) under their nests. Storing food right by their beds means chipmunks do not have to travel far to get breakfast, especially in the cold of winter.

Because there are so many animals in the forest, they compete with each other for food. Over time, animals have developed several ways to compete. One is defending their stores of food. Chipmunks defend their all-important winter food piles with loud *chuck-chuck* calls if squirrels or any other animals try to steal them. Chipmunks forage in the morning, while red squirrels forage mostly in late afternoon. By

It is pure luck that Warren Woods survives at all, because everything around it was cleared for farming in the late 1800s. A forward-thinking storekeeper named E. K. Warren had made his fortune by selling under-wear made from turkey feathers! He decided to use his money to buy and preserve Warren Woods— an idea far ahead of its time.

Moose have found plenty of food on Isle Royale. Wolves are the only serious threat to their population.

choosing different times of the day for activity, each animal has as much time as possible to find its own food without the other's interference. In fact, this is one reason why some animals are active at night, while others are active during the day.

Superior Surroundings

Isle Royale National Park is a 210-square-mile (545-sq-km) island in the middle of Lake Superior. The island is covered by forests of white spruce, balsam fir, white birch, and aspen. On the parts of the island that have warmer slopes and thicker soils, there are hardwood forests of sugar maple and yellow birch. Isle Royale is especially beautiful in spring and summer, exploding in the colors of more than two dozen kinds of orchids. Animals also live here. Loons search for fish on the island's beaches. Foxes chase hares and squirrels—their favorite foods—through the forests, while beavers build their dams along winding creeks and bubbling brooks.

Because it is an island, Isle Royale is isolated from plant and animal communities on the mainland. Islands are intriguing to **ecologists** because each is an ecological laboratory, where relationships among species are in delicate balance and can change quite rapidly if anything disturbs that equilibrium. Ecologists have been studying Isle Royale continuously for decades. It is the site of the longest-running mammal study in the United States, a study of the connections between two species—wolves and moose, predators and prey.

Moose swam to Isle Royale from Canada in the early 1900s. They found plenty of vegetation, including balsam fir trees, which they love to eat. A food chain was established between the balsam fir, which uses energy from the sun to make food, and the moose, which feeds on the upper branches. Balsam fir can make up more than half of a moose's diet in winter. On the island, the moose population grew. Sometimes the moose had trouble finding food because of heavy snowfall, droughts, fires, or overgrazing that reduced the supply. At those times, their population would decline. But in general, Isle Royale was a safe place for moose because they had no predators. Then, during an especially cold winter, probably in 1950, a male and a female wolf walked across the frozen lake from Canada and discovered an island filled with food.

Within ten years, the population of wolves on Isle Royale had grown to 20. At the same time, there were more than 600 moose. Scientists who began their study in 1958 had many questions about these predator and prey populations. They wanted to understand whether the numbers of wolves and moose would vary over time. And if the numbers did vary, how and why did that happen? One important finding of the Isle Royale researchers is that the numbers of wolves and moose do change over time. In one boom year, for example, nearly 1,700 moose were counted. In a different year, the wolf population peaked at 50 before beginning a crash to only 12.

The wolf and moose populations influence each other, though the connections are not straightforward—when there are plenty of moose, there are not necessarily plenty of wolves. Wolves need to find moose that they can kill—the weak, ill, old, or very young. When such vulnerable moose are rare, wolf numbers may drop. When wolf numbers drop, moose calf survival may increase. When there are more moose, wolf numbers eventually grow again.

Because wolves are predators of moose on Isle Royale, their populations are linked.

When scientists add balsam firs to the food chain study, there are more questions to ask and patterns to detect. The Isle Royale research continues, hoping to draw a more complete picture of the ways predators and prey interact through time.

Forests Forever?

Habitat destruction has greatly altered the forested shores. Logging for shipbuilding, construction, and papermaking has destroyed most of the dense forests. Logging in this area was mainly done by clear-cutting, or removing all the trees from an area at once. These naked lands no longer support many animals or have the valuable services only trees can provide. Trees are the start of many food chains. They capture and cycle soil and nutrients in roots and use those nutrients to grow branches, leaves, and bark. Insects, birds, and mammals get the nutrients by feeding on different parts of the tree. Without trees to anchor the soil and soak up those nutrients, erosion has increased dramatically, washing nutrients directly into the lake. This means that sedimentation and nutrient levels in the lakes rise beyond what they can absorb—causing lake habitat to suffer.

Logging removed the old forests, and acid rain affects the much younger forests here today. Acid rain is formed when pollutants from burning fossil fuels, such as oil or coal, rise into the air and mix with water vapor. The water vapor, as clouds, carries pollutants far from their sources and then deposits them in raindrops into the lakes and over the forests. This acidic rain leaves layers of pollutants on trees and other plants. When acid rain hits trees regularly, they lose their leaves and are unable to photosynthesize. Increased acid in the soil also reduces the soil's ability to keep nutrients, which run off into lake waters.

Fortunately, people realized what was happening and took action. The U.S. government passed the Clean Air Act in 1977. This law limits the amount of pollution factories can release into the air. The Clean Water Act regulates what kinds of pollutants go into the water. And the Great Lakes Water Quality Agreement asks everyone around the lakes to work together in thinking about how to replant forests and stop pollution.

How Healthy Is Your Water?

You can evaluate the health of your water by conducting a survey on your nearest stream or pond. Prepare yourself by wearing old shoes and clothes that you do not mind getting wet. Make sure you are going somewhere safe; take a friend with you.

Materials:

- clipboard
- pencil
- paper or notebook
- plastic cup
- litmus paper
- small net
- plastic tray or plate

1. At the stream, look around the banks. Do you see trash? What kind? Where does it come from? Make a list of synthetic (manufactured) items you see around the stream. If there is a lot of trash, you may have a reason to worry about your stream's health.

2. Pick up some soil near the edge. What color is it? Do you see any insects or worms in it? If you do, that means the soil is healthy. Draw a picture of the creatures you see. What does the soil feel like? It should be a little damp. If it is too dry, that means few plants can grow around the stream to prevent runoff from polluting the water.

3. Scoop up some water in your cup and look closely at it. What color is the water? Healthy water should be fairly clear. If it is very murky, there may be too much erosion running into the stream. Does the water have a smell? A strong smell may tell you there is a nearby source of pollution.

4. Are there plants or animals in the water? Hold your net in the water for a couple of minutes and let the water flow through it. Then take out your net and examine what you have caught on a plastic plate or tray. If you see three or more different kinds of small insects, your water is fairly healthy. If you see fewer, or none, it means the stream may be sick.

5. Scoop some water into your cup and dip a piece of litmus paper into the cup to see how acidic the water is. The pH scale measures acidity. Pure water has a pH of seven. If your litmus paper shows a pH number less than seven, that means it is acidic, and acidity makes water a more difficult habitat for plants and animals. Record the pH in your journal.

6. Sit for a while near the stream or pond and watch carefully. Do you see any wildlife? What kind? What is it doing? Healthy ponds and streams have lots of wildlife.

7. Record all your observations on your paper or notebook. If you can, return another day and do the same thing again. Share your information with your family or classmates. If you found your stream to be unhealthy, try to think of ways you might be able to help it get well.

The Future of the Lakes

*T*he Great Lakes ecosystem is always changing. Floods alter the coastline. Beavers chew down trees to build dams. Populations of fish grow and shrink. Tree fall and open gaps in the forest for new growth. These natural changes are constant; some happen quickly, others slowly. Animals and plants adapt. But despite the lakes' huge size and great diversity of species, their story in the past century has been one of fighting against the impact of humans. Relationships among plants, animals, water, air, and soil are sensitive to change, and the changes humans have brought have been swift and broad. This speed means that animal and plant communities have little chance to adapt and are often driven, at the least, from their habitats. At worst, species are driven to extinction. Once gone, species cannot be recovered.

Since the time of the first human settlement, the lakes have endured the effects of ever-increasing numbers of people. These effects are many. We have pumped excess nutrients into the lakes, causing eutrophication. We have harvested too much ore, drinking water, and peat moss. We have deforested miles and miles of land, removing essential soil anchors from the shores and causing erosion.

Logging on the shores of the Great Lakes has led to increased erosion and excessive nutrients in the lakes.

We have introduced exotic species, such as the zebra mussel, which have disrupted balances among native species. We have poisoned fish and birds with toxic pollutants.

Every species in an ecosystem interacts with many others. Some pollutants can become magnified through bioaccumulation in the food chain. Small amounts of toxins concentrate in those animals higher on the food chain and can cause life-threatening problems. Eggshell thinning in eagles, tumors on fish, and crossed bills on cormorants are examples of these toxic effects. There are numerous species that are already gravely threatened in the Great Lakes, including the piping plover, the lake trout, and some entire communities. Humans are not immune. As the top predators in many food chains, we know that toxins affect us as well. Though the evidence is still being collected, scientists have discovered problems in the memory skills of babies whose mothers ate contaminated fish from Lake Michigan.

Species and communities can recover if we give them the chance. There are many things that humans can do to help make sure that organisms and their environments continue. One action is to study biological communities in order to learn more about them. Only by understanding the relationships among species and the

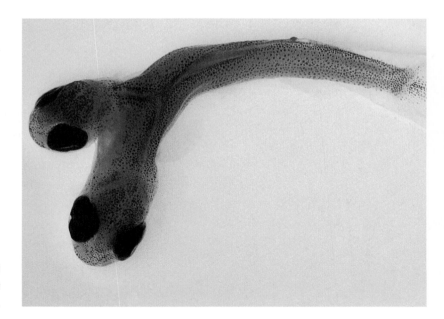

Toxic pollutants in the lakes have led to genetic mutations such as this.

ways nutrients and chemicals cycle through these living communities can we know enough to help. It is also important to monitor agricultural techniques for clearing land and applying pesticides. These practices can cause erosion and may increase nutrients and chemicals in the water. Less harmful farming methods need to be discussed and implemented in ways that are economically valuable to farmers.

It is also important to continue monitoring and improving industrial processes that release toxins directly or indirectly into the water. The pulp and paper industry released highly toxic mercury into lake waters until scientists found out how toxic it actually was. Then paper factories were able to change their process to avoid this pollutant. Under new laws, industrial practices are continually adapting to reduce toxic pollution.

Sustainable development is an important concept for the Great Lakes. If we overfish, there will soon be nothing left to harvest. If we build too many homes, the water we depend on will no longer be safe to drink. It is important to understand limits, have respect for the future, and leave the ecosystem as we would want those in the future to find it. The U.S. and Canadian governments are cooperating to improve and restore the ecosystem. Research by universities and government agencies contributes to our understanding of ecosystem relationships and habitat restoration projects. The return of the cormorant and the bald eagle are signs that people can help the system recover.

Astronauts report that the Great Lakes are the only inland ecological feature visible with the naked eye from the moon. It would be a wonderful thing to report that they are still as beautiful up close as they are from that great distance.

Glossary

adaptations features that help a living organism survive in its environment. A beaver has adaptations for life in the water. It has thick, waterproof fur, webbed feet for swimming, and transparent eyelids like goggles for seeing underwater.

benthic organisms organisms that live at the bottom of a lake or stream. In Lake Erie, bottom-feeding whitefish are benthic organisms that eat dead plankton from the lake's floor and use the nutrients for energy.

bioaccumulation the process by which small amounts of chemicals concentrate in the bodies of animals at the tops of food chains.

blowout dune a large bowl-like cavity created in a weak section of a dune when wind or fire destroys the vegetation that once anchored the sands.

canopy the top layer of the forest, where the leaves of the tallest trees are found.

carnivorous describes a meat-eating plant or animal.

climate long-term weather patterns of a region.

community all of the organisms that live together and interact in a particular environment.

conifer evergreens trees that grow needles, which they keep year-round, and store their seeds in cones.

deciduous trees trees that lose their leaves in the fall.

decomposers an organism that gets its energy by breaking down dead organisms. Fungi and many types of bacteria are decomposers that feed on dead plants and animals.

dunes stretches of sandy landscape formed when wind and water currents drive sand and sediment upland from the beaches.

ecologists scientists who study the relationships among species and their environment.

ecology the study of relationships between organisms and their environment.

ecosystem a community of plants and animals tied together by the physical, chemical, and biological cycles of their environment.

emergent plants plants that grow with their roots and bases in wet soil or water for part or all of their lives.

environment all of the conditions and influences surrounding an organism. For example, the Great Lakes environment includes water, land, temperature, plants, and animals.

eskers long, narrow ridges formed by glacial movements.

eutrophication the process by which dead and dying organisms use up oxygen in the water.

exotic species a species that is not native to the area in which it now lives.

food chain a series of organisms in a community in which each organism eats the one below it. In the Great Lakes, zooplankton eat phytoplankton, trout eat smelt, and ospreys eat trout. When an osprey dies, decomposers take it apart, and its nutrients return to the water or soil to begin the chain again.

habitat the place that has all the living and nonliving things an organism needs to live and grow. Lake Erie is the walleye's habitat.

kames cone-shaped mounds left from glacial debris.

moraines massive ridges formed from glacial meltwater debris.

niche an organism's space and role within its habitat.

photosynthesis the process by which plants harness the sun's energy to make their own food.

phytoplankton tiny floating plants. Also known as algae, they create their own energy from the sun and provide food for many other organisms in the food chain.

predator an animal that kills other animals for food.

species a group of similar organisms that can breed with each other.

submergent plants plants that have their stems, leaves, and roots mostly underwater. In the Great Lakes, two common examples are pondweeds and bladderworts. They are highly sensitive and can gather light for photosynthesis even in murky water.

succession the process by which one group of organisms provides the conditions for another group of organisms.

surface runoff water falling on land that returns to lakes by flowing over the surface of the land rather than being absorbed by the soil.

tributaries streams and rivers leading to larger bodies of water.

understory the lower level of the forest where shorter trees are blocked by the taller trees of the canopy.

water cycle process by which water is transformed from vapor in the atmosphere to precipitation on land and water surfaces and ultimately back into the air.

wetland an area where the water level lies above the surface for all or part of the year.

zooplankton tiny floating animals.

Further Exploration

Books and Articles

Blocksma, Mary. *The Fourth Coast*. New York: Penguin Books, 1995.

Cobb, Charles E. "The Great Lakes' Troubled Waters." *National Geographic*, July 1987.

Eliot, John L. "Isle Royale: A North Woods Park Primeval." *National Geographic*, April 1985.

Ellis, William D. *Land of the Inland Seas*. Palo Alto, CA: American West Publishing Company, 1974.

Holling, Clancy. *Paddle-to-the-Sea*. Boston: Houghton Mifflin, 1969.

Leopold, Aldo. *A Sand County Almanac*. New York: Ballantine Books, 1966.

Staub, Frank. *America's Wetlands*. Minneapolis, MN: Carolrhoda Books, Inc., 1995.

Strutin, Michele. *The Smithsonian Guides to Natural America: The Great Lakes*. Washington, DC: Smithsonian Books, 1996.

U.S. Environmental Protection Agency. *The Great Lakes: An Environmental Atlas and Resource Book*. Chicago: Great Lakes National Program Office, 1995.

Wilson, E. O. *The Diversity of Life*. New York: W. W. Norton and Company, 1992.

On the Internet

http://www.great-lakes.net
http://epaserver.ciesin.org/glreis
http://www.epa.gov/glnpo

Organizations

The Nature Conservancy
Great Lakes
Program Office
8 South Michigan Avenue
Suite 2301
Chicago, IL 60603
(312) 759-8017

National Wildlife
Federation
Great Lakes Natural
Resource Center
506 E. Liberty 2nd Fl.
Ann Arbor, MI
48104-2210
(734) 769-3351

Environment Canada,
Ontario Region
4905 Dufferin Street
Downsview, Ontario
M3H 5T4
(416) 739-4826

Index

Page numbers for illustrations are in **boldface**.